Album of Violin Pieces

This book of violin pieces provides a wide variety of style, color, and character, including the most noteworthy compositions in musical history, all carefully revised and edited. While the student will find the contents of this book interesting and invaluable for recreation and practice, the virtuoso will recognize this set of selections as being indispensible to his library. Includes piano accompaniment.

Order No. AM 40056
International Standard Book Number: 0.8256.2006.6

Exclusive Distributors:
Music Sales Corporation
257 Park Avenue South, New York, NY 10010 USA
Music Sales Limited
8/9 Frith Street, London W1D 3JB England
Music Sales Pty. Limited
120 Rothschild Street, Rosebery, Sydney, NSW 2018, Australia

Printed in the United States of America by
Vicks Lithograph and Printing Corporation

Amsco Publications
New York/London/Paris/Sydney/Copenhagen/Madrid

Contents

ABOUT THE COMPOSER....

BACH, JOHANN SEBASTIAN. . . . . (1685-1750)
The consummate genius of the great Bach family and one of the greatest figures in music history. The total amount of his work is prodigious, not only in bulk but in depth of content and orginality of form.

BEETHOVEN, LUDWIG VAN. . . . . (1770-1827)
Wrote nine symphonies, quartets, sonatas, masses, concerti, one opera and numerous small pieces including songs. Many of his best works were written after he had become deaf in 1801.

BOHM, CARL . . . . (1844-1920)
Prolific composer of songs and violin music which achieved wide popularity. Known perhaps for his song "Calm As The Night."

BRAGA, GAETANO . . . . (1829-1907)
Italian cellist. Wrote eight operas, instrumental, vocal and religious music.

BRAHMS, JOHANNES . . . . (1833-1897)
One of the great masters of 19th century music. Among his works are 4 symphonies, 2 piano concerti, chamber music, songs and a violin concerto.

CHAMINADE, CECIL . . . . (1857-1944)
French composer and pianist. Wrote many popular characteristic piano pieces, songs, two orchestral suites and one opera, "La Sevillane."

CUI, CAESAR . . . . (1835-1918)
Distinguished Russian composer. He excelled in lyric characterization, in delicate and tender effects, neatness and conciseness of structure. He was stronger vocally than orchestrally but none of his operas attained great success.

DRDLA, FRANZ . . . . (1868-1944)
His outstanding popularity as a composer of violin pieces partially obscures the fact that he himself was a violinist of brilliance and distinction. Two concert tours in America, however, established his virtuoso quality in the public mind. He has written over 300 works.

DVOŘÁK, ANTON. . . . . (1841-1904)
Celebrated Bohemian composer. His gifts for melody, for rhythm and for harmonic combinations were extraordinarily great and highly original.

DRIGO, RICARDO. . . . . (1846-1930)
Composer of great talent especially as to melody and wealth of emotion. The "Serenade" is probably the most popular of his light compositions.

ELGAR, EDWARD . . . . (1857-1934)
Eminent English composer. His marked orginality of conception and mastery of expression led him to a rapid growth of remarkable renown. His compositions include many orchestral works, chamber music and vocal pieces.

GLUCK, CHRISTOPHER. . . . . (1714-1787)
Distinguished Bavarian composer, becoming at length the leader in the reform of the opera that was the foundation of modern styles. His stage works totaled about 100. Also several overtures, choral settings and a few songs.

GODARD, BENJAMIN . . . . (1849-1895)
Eminent French composer. His works show a fine instinct for orchestral color and much graceful inspiration.

GOUNOD, CHARLES . . . . (1818-1893)
Renowned French composer. Wrote many operas of which "Faust" is the most popular. Also many sacred, choral and instrumental works. All his work is marked by poetic sentiment, nobility of conception and great dexterity in instrumentation.

GRIEG, EDVARD. . . . . (1843-1906)
Norwegian pianist, composer of exceptional ability. Best known of his compositions are his piano concerto, string quartette, many Norwegian songs and the famous "Peer Gynt" suite.

HANDEL, GEORG FRIEDRICH . . . . (1685-1759)
Composer, orchestra conductor and concert organist. Wrote a number of operas and oratorios. Was a prolific writer of all forms of sacred music. Two outstanding compositions were the "Largo" and oratorio "Messiah," which is said to have met with the greatest success ever accorded a musical composition.

MASSENET, JULES . . . . (1842-1912)
Eminent French composer. His facile and melodious style was early acquired and remained throughout his long career. He won the popular interest always with the aid of fine workmanship and versatility of subject.

MENDELSSOHN, FELIX. . . . . (1809-1847)
Was a learned man in the arts and sciences as well as music. Began writing at the age of eleven. Best known works are "Songs Without Words," "Midsummernight's Dream," and the oratorio "Elijah."

MOSZKOWSKI, MORITZ. . . . . (1854-1925)
A concert pianist of note and composer of many musical masterpieces outstanding among which are the "Serenata" and "Guitarre."

POLDINI, EDUARD . . . . (1869-1957)
Hungarian composer of note. Wrote the comic opera "Der Vagabond und die Prinzessin," several fairy plays for children and numerous instrumental pieces.

RAFF, JOSEPH JOACHIM. . . . . (1822-1882)
Distinguished Swiss composer. Was intimately associated with Liszt, Mendelssohn and Von Bulow and their circle.

RUBENSTEIN, ANTON. . . . . (1829-1894)
One of the finest pianists of his time. His piano compositions, songs, symphonies and oratorios are marked examples of grace, dignity and refinement.

SARASATE, PABLO DE . . . . (1844-1908)
Eminent Spanish composer and violinist. He wrote only for violin.

SCHUBERT, FRANZ. . . . . (1797-1828)
A composer of exceptional genius. Living under the shadow of his great contemporary, Beethoven, he was unknown to fame and his works known only to his intimate circle of friends. Although he wrote in many forms, his great contribution is associated with the art of song.

SCHUMANN, ROBERT . . . . (1810-1856)
Life devoted to music as a pianist, composer and music editor. Wrote many songs, sonatas, symphonies, fantasies, concertos, etc. Franz Liszt did much to popularize his compositions by playing them frequently in his concerts.

Souvenir

FRANZ DRDLA

p
p
p
mf
f
rit.
mf rit.
p
Poco vivo
f
Poco vivo
mf
p
ritard.

pp a tempo
ppp a tempo
p
animato poco a poco
cresc.
f accel.
rall.
p a tempo
f accel.
rall.
a tempo p

Sul A
cresc.
mf
f rit.
p
a tempo
sul A
rit.
a tempo
pp
mf
f
meno
r.h.
l.h.
a tempo
dim.
pizz.
(pizz.)
p rit.
mf a tempo

Dancing Doll

(POUPEE VALSANTE)

ED. POLDINI

sempre p
mf
8va ad lib.
poco rit.
Tempo I
mf
Tempo I
stacc.
p
poco rit.
mf
p
pp delicatamente
pp
(Melody) mf

sul G
fz
p
p
p
dim.
pp
dim.
ppp

Two Guitars

Russian Gypsy Folk Song

Andante con moto

pizz.

p

Andante con moto

p

arco

mf

mf

poco piu mosso

f

(a little faster)

fz

f

poco piu mosso

meno mosso
rit.
a tempo
p
R.H.
Moderato
poco a poco accel. e cresc.
mf a tempo
Moderato
poco a poco accel. e cresc.
a tempo
mf
Presto
accel.
f
Presto
f
Allegro (little slower)
ff
Allegro (little slower)
mf
pizz.
ff
mf

Andante con moto
pizz.
p
Andante con moto
p
Andante (slower)
arco
Andante (slower)
un poco accel.
un poco accel.
mf
rall.
f
mp a tempo
mf
rall.
f
mp a tempo
Moderato
p
poco accel.
Moderato
p
poco accel.

Poco più mosso
pizz.
Poco più mosso
arco
Moderato
a tempo
Moderato
Presto
accel.
Presto
Allegro (little slower)
Allegro (little slower)
Presto
arco
pizz.
Presto

Zigeunerweisen

P. DE SARASATE

Lento
arco
f con molto passione
rall.
3
Lento
p
rall.
p
rit.
pp
f ritenuto espressivo
4
pp
mf ritenuto espressivo
gliss.
rit.
string.
rit.
pp
f a tempo
5
pp
rit.
pp
ad libitum
rit.
veloce
molto riten.
pp
glissando
pp
riten.

loco
a tempo
dim.
gliss.
rit.
6
pp rit.
rit.
a tempo
7
rit.
(legg.)
rit.
8
f a tempo
pp
f rit.
misurato

a tempo
rit.
tr♯
rit.
9
pp
Un poco più lento
*) con sordino
molto espressivo
Un poco più lento
(espressivo)
10
pp
poco marcato
pp
11
pp
ppp
rit.
pp
12
ritard
a tempo
(poco rit.)
13
ritard
ppp

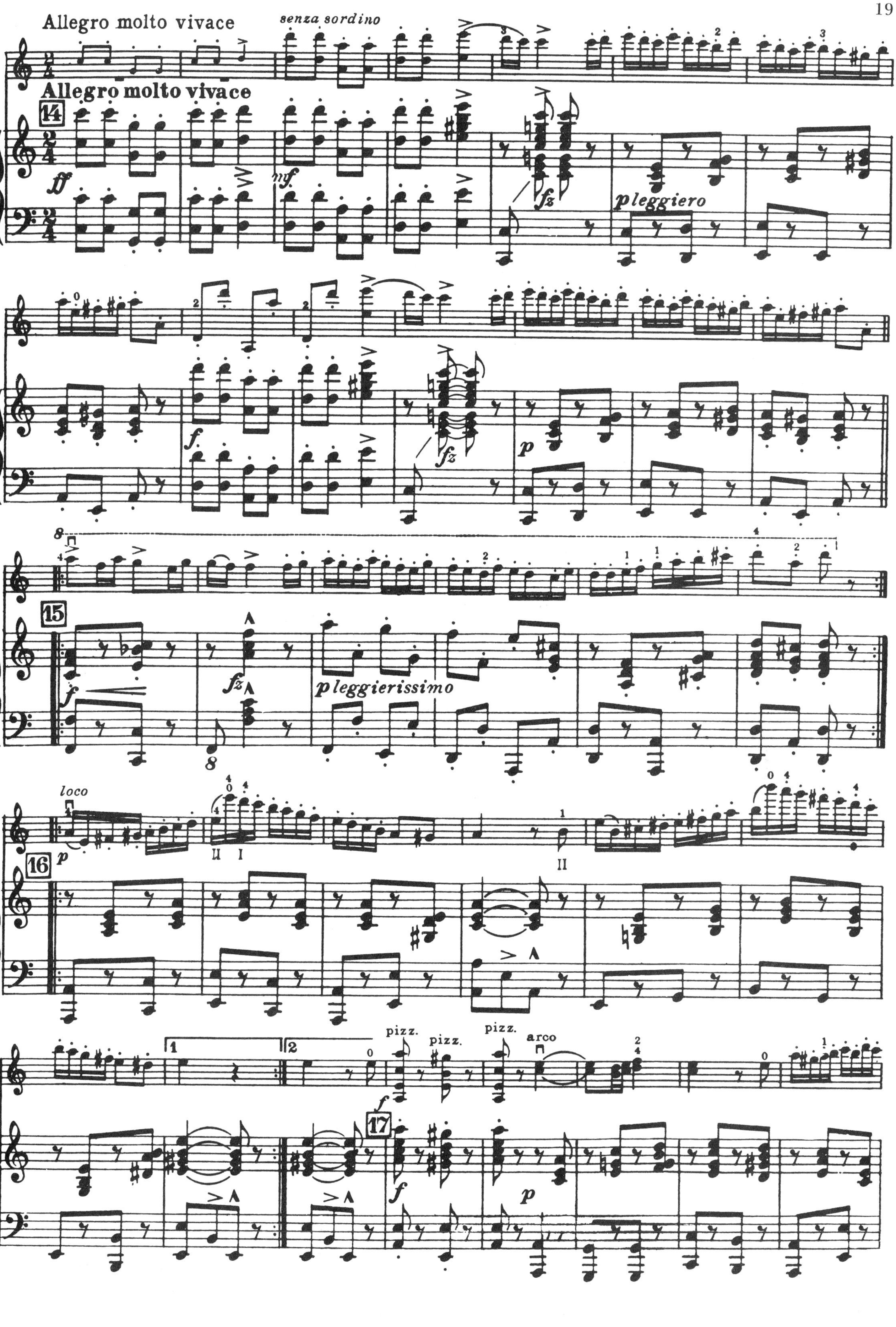
Allegro molto vivace
senza sordino
Allegro molto vivace
14
ff
mf
fz
p leggiero
f
fz
p
8
15
f
fz
p leggierissimo
8
loco
16
p
1
2
pizz.
pizz.
pizz.
arco
17
f
f
p

loco
pizz.
pizz.
pizz.
arco
f
p
18
pp poco più
19
20
p
fz

21
fz
arco
f
IV
22
pp leggierissimo e staccato
pizz.
arco
23
f
p
loco
f animato
24
f animato
più animato
cresc.
f
ff

Serenade

FRANZ DRDLA

A
rit.
a tempo
rit.
a tempo
f
rall.
f
rall.
(lower notes may be omitted)
f a tempo
f a tempo
rit.
rit.

pp
a tempo
a tempo
pp
cresc.
cresc.
f
rit.
f rit.
poco animato
p
f a tempo
a tempo
p
p
8
f
mf
pp
f poco animato
f
rit.

p a tempo
p a tempo
rit.
p
p a tempo
cresc.
cresc.
f
f
rit.
rit.
mf
a tempo
f a tempo
rit.
rit.
a tempo
p a tempo
tr
tr
f
rit.
rit.
p
pizz.
f a tempo
f a tempo

Spanish Dance

M. MOSZKOWSKI, Op. 12, No. 1

f
mf
p
mp
mp
f

f
p
p e grazioso
p e grazioso
marcato
marcato
p
p

marcato
marcato

Air For The G-string

J. S. BACH

p cresc.
p
cresc.
f
f
pp dolciss.
tr
p cresc.
p
f
pp
cresc.
f
pp
f
dim.
f
poco rit.
tr
a tempo
molto rit.
a tempo
dim.
e
poco rit.
molto rit.

Träumerei

R. SCHUMANN, Op. 15, No. 7

p a tempo
p a tempo
rit.
mf
rit.
a tempo
a tempo
rit.
rit.
p
p

Salut d'Amour

(LOVE'S GREETING)

E. ELGAR, Op. 12

Harm.
cresc. molto
rit.
p a tempo
rit.
p a tempo
dolce
cresc.
p
string.
cresc.
cresc.
ff
string.
p accel.
cresc.
p accel.
cresc.
f
rit.
f rit.
Sul G
ff
p rit. molto
dim.
rit. molto
Tempo più molto
pp
Tempo più molto
poco rit.
p
rall.
poco rit.
p
rall.
rall.

Humoreske

ANTON DVOŘÁK, Op. 101, No. 7

A
rit.
rit.
A
A
E
rit.
Un più mosso
f
rit. colla Solo
Un più mosso
f
dim.
f
fz
D
dim.
poco rit.
dim.
f
poco rit.
dim.
mf
poco rit.
f
mf
poco rit.
f

E
A
pp
p arpeggiato
A
A
E
rit.
rit.
a tempo
a tempo
f
f
A
p
pp
very soft
p
pp
very soft
D
rit.
rit.
ppp
ppp

The Rain
(PERPETUUM MOBILE)

CARL BOHM

cresc.

R.H.

dim.

sempre staccato

p
f
mf
cresc.
ff

Melody in F

ANTON RUBINSTEIN

mf
f
Sul D
mf
Sul G
dim.
dim.
p
stringendo
p
p

mf
mf
f
Sul D
mf
f
mf
Sul G
dim.
dim.
p
p
tr
tr

f
cresc.
cresc.
ff
ff
f
mf
mf
f
dim.
dim.
pp
pp
8

Ave Maria
(Meditation on Bach, Prelude in C)

BACH-GOUNOD

cresc.
cresc.
dim.
dim.
pp
pp
creso
cresc.
pp
pp
creso.
cresc.
cresc.
cresc.
dim.
dim.
creso.
cresc.
en
en
do
do
molto
molto

f
dim.
p
cresc.
f
dim.
p
cresc.
molto
f
piu f
tutta forza
molto
f
piu f
tutta forza
molto
maestoso
p
cresc.
cresc.

pp
cresc.
pp
cresc.
dim.
p
pp
cresc.
pp
cresc.
cresc.
dim.
p
cresc.

en
do
molto
en
do
molto
f
dim.
p
cresc.
f
dim.
p
cresc.
molto
f
piu f
tutta forza
molto
f
piu f
tutta forza
molto
maestoso
f
p
f
dim.

Cavatina

JOACHIM RAFF

smorzando
D
A
cresc.
A
A
cresc.
cresc.
sul G

Grandioso
Grandioso
rinfz.
rinfz.
ff string.
ff stringendo
a tempo
a tempo
smorzando
sul G
cong
cong

Minuet in G

L. VAN BEETHOVEN

Minuet D.C.

ANDANTE

C. W. GLUCK

Anitra's Dance
(PEER GYNT)

EDWARD GRIEG

arco
p
p
p
dolce
pp
pp
fp

cresc.
fp
cresc.
f
f
dim.
dim.
poco rit.
p
a tempo
p
pizz.
p
pp
pizz.
f
f
arco
pp
pp
pp

Romance

A. RUBINSTEIN, Op. 44

p
rall.
rall.
p a tempo
p a tempo
cresc.
rit.
rit.

a tempo
f a tempo
p
cresc.
sul A
leggiero
pp

Serenade
(LES MILLIONS D'ARLEQUIN)

R. DRIGO

p
sempre p
cresc.
cresc.
poco rit.
poco rit.
p piu sustenuto
pp
cresc.
cresc.

f espressivo
tremolo
sempre p
Sul A
p espressivo
pp
Sul A
tranquillo
Sul E
sempre p
8
sempre pp
dim.
a poco
ppp

Pizzicato
(SYLVIA BALLET)

LEO DELIBES

sf rit. - - - p a tempo
rit.
p a tempo
accel.
cresc.
f
f
arco
f ben sostenuto
p
arco

Un poco anima
mf
pizz.
arco
pizz.
arco
Un poco anima
mf
cresc. poco a poco animato cresc.
cresc.
f
ff
ff
ff

Angel's Serenade
(LA SERENATA)

G. BRAGA

p
pp
il canto ben marcato
cresc.
cresc.
mf affrettando
poco più animato

cresc.
f
cresc.
f
Tempo I
Tempo I
p
sul A

cresc.
cresc.
tr
mf
con anima
rall.
p
rall.
pp a tempo
pp

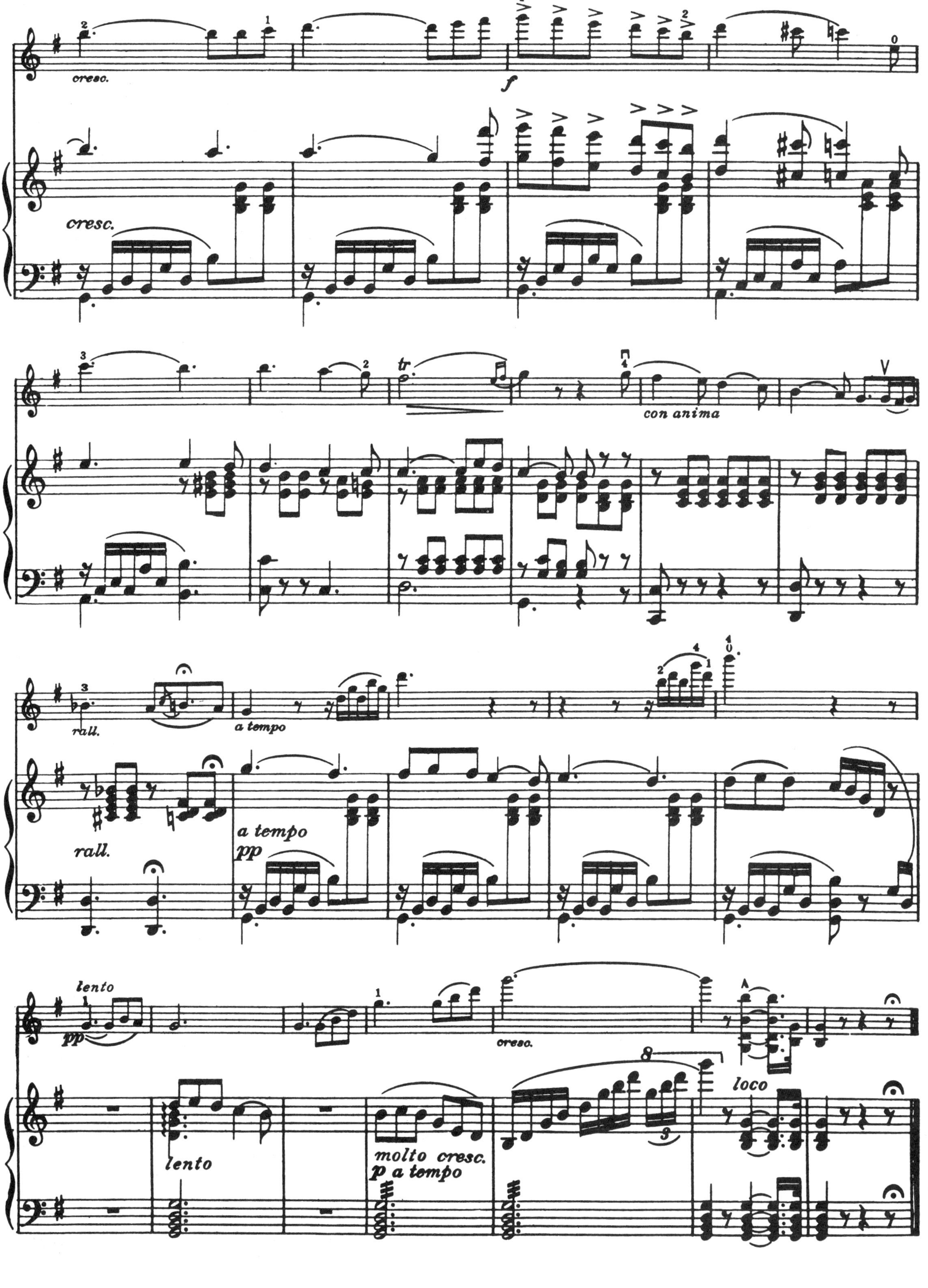

cresc.

f

cresc.

con anima

rall.

a tempo

rall.

a tempo

pp

lento

cresc.

lento

molto cresc.

p a tempo

loco

Largo

G. F. HANDEL

f
p
mf
f
ff
pp
ppp
ff
f
p
ff
pp
ff
rit.
rit.
p

Élégie

J. MASSENET

Berceuse
(From "JOCELYN")

B. GODARD

Andante
Andante
(cross left hand over right)
l.h.
pp con sordini
cresc.
sul A
f
f
rall.
pp
a tempo
a tempo
marcato
p
f
pp
rall.
pp
Quasi recit
mf

a tempo
tranquillo
cresc.
p a tempo
pp
rall.
dim.
colla parte
Andantino
Andantino
(cross left hand over right)
l.h.
con sordini
sul A
cresc.
rall.
marcato
f

Hungarian Dance
No. 5

J. BRAHMS

p leggiero
sf
p
sf
f
sf
sf
sf
p poco rit.
sf a tempo f
sf
p poco rit.
f
8
Vivace
sf
f
Vivace
sf

arco
pizz.
arco
pizz.
p poco rit.
a tempo
leggiero
p
a tempo
p poco rit.
a tempo
a tempo
p poco rit.
p a tempo
poco rit.
p poco rit.
a tempo
poco rit.
p a tempo
f fieramente
a tempo

p leggiero
p
sf
f
p poco rit.
a tempo
ff

Scarf Dance

C. CHAMINADE

cresc.
p
cresc.
mf
dim. e rit.
p a tempo ma rubato
dim. e rit.
pp a tempo ma rubato
f
mf
dim. - p - et - rit. - - - pp
dim. - p - et - rit. - - pp

Spring Song
(SONGS WITHOUT WORDS, NO. 30)

F. MENDELSSOHN

cresc.
p
cresc.
f
fz
dim.
dim.
f
sf
dim.
p
f
dim.
cresc.
p dolce
cresc.
cresc.
p
cresc.

dim.
dim.
f
dim.
grazioso
pp
p
pp
cresc.
cresc.
f

dim
f
dim.
p
p dolce
cresc.
p dolce
grazioso
dim.
pp
pizz.
pp
leggiero

Serenata

M. MOSZKOWSKI, Op. 15

cresc.
a tempo
f
rubato
sfz
cresc.
a tempo
rubato
dim.
dim.
molto rit.
gliss.
p a tempo
molto rit.
a tempo
rit.
rit.
p a tempo
rit.
pp
a tempo
rit.
pp

Orientale
(THE KALEIDESCOPE)

CESAR CUI, Op. 50

pizz.
arco
pizz.
arco
pizz.
arco
pizz.
arco
pizz.
arco
p
cresc.
p cresc.
mf
p
pp
rit.
a tempo
mf
rit.
p a tempo
cresc.
f
pizz.
arco
pizz.
arco
pizz.
arco
pizz.
arco
pizz.
ppp
pp
ppp

Serenade

FRANZ SCHUBERT

f
mf
mf
pp
p
pp
p
p
pp

decrescendo
decrescendo
dimin.